NOW YOU CAN READ.....
ISAAC AND REBEKAH

STORY RETOLD BY ARLENE C. ROURKE

ILLUSTRATED BY GWEN GREEN

Published by Rourke Publications, Inc., P.O. Box 3328, Vero Beach, Florida 32964. Copyright © 1985 by Rourke Publications, Inc. All copyrights reserved. No part of this book may be reproduced in any form without written permission from the publisher. Printed in the United States of America.

The Publishers acknowledge permission from Brimax Books for the use of the name "Now You Can Read" and "Large Type For First Readers" which identify Brimax Now You Can Read series.

Library of Congress Cataloging in Publication Data

Rourke, Arlene, 1944-
  Isaac & Rebekah.

  Summary: A retelling of the Old Testament story of how Isaac came to marry Rebekah and found the twelve tribes of Israel.
    1. Isaac (Biblical patriarch)—Juvenile literature.
2. Rebekah (Biblical matriarch)—Juvenile literature.
3. Bible. O.T.—Biography—Juvenile literature.
[1. Isaac (Biblical patriarch) 2. Rebekah (Biblical matriarch) 3. Bible stories—O.T.] I. Title.
II. Title: Isaac and Rebekah.
BS580.I67R68 1985   222'.1109505   85-19309
ISBN 0-86625-316-5

GROLIER ENTERPRISES CORP.

NOW YOU CAN READ. . . .
ISAAC AND REBEKAH

Long, long ago, a man named Abram
and his wife Sarai lived in a city
called Ur. One day, Abram heard the
voice of God. God told him to leave
Ur and go to the land of Canaan.

Because Abram and Sarai were good people, they did as God told them to do. They packed their belongings and brought their servants and cattle to Canaan.

Many years passed, Abram and Sarai grew old. Again, Abram heard the voice of God. "Abram, you will be the father of a great nation," the voice said.

"Lord, how can this be? Sarai and I are old and we have no children," Abram pleaded.

"You and Sarai will have a son," God said. "He will be called Isaac. You will change your name to Abraham and Sarai will be called Sarah."

Just as God promised, a son was born to Abraham and Sarah. He was the answer to their prayers. They were very happy!

Isaac was the only child that Abraham and Sarah had. They saw to it that he had good food to eat and warm clothes to wear. They talked with him and played with him. He always made them laugh. They loved him dearly.

One day, Abraham again heard the voice of God.

"Do you love me, Abraham?" God asked.

"Of course, my Lord. I love you with all my heart," Abraham answered.

"Then you must prove it." God said. "Give me the dearest thing that you have."

When he heard this, Abraham's heart sank. He knew what God wanted. The dearest thing he had was Isaac. God was asking Abraham to sacrifice Isaac to Him. Abraham was heart-broken. He knew that he must do what God asked.

Next morning, Abraham woke Isaac up early. He did not tell him what God had said. "Get up," he told Isaac. "We have to go somewhere."

They went into
the mountains.
At last, they
came to a
lonely place
very high up.
Abraham lit a
fire and built
an altar.
"God has called
for a sacrifice,"
Abraham said.

With that, he pulled out his knife and reached for Isaac. Suddenly the voice of God could be heard all over the mountain.

"Abraham, do not hurt your son. I would not ask such a great sacrifice of you. You have proved your faith. Take Isaac home."

Abraham was so happy! He hugged his son and kissed him. He had not been so happy since Isaac was born.

In time, Isaac grew to manhood. He was a fine, young man. One day, a terrible thing happened. Isaac's beloved mother, Sarah, died. Abraham and Isaac were very sad.

Abraham sat alone and thought.
"I am an old man, but Isaac is young.
He must find a wife."

Abraham called his trusted servant, Eliezer, to him. "Go to Haran, the country of my birth," Abraham said. "Find a good wife for my son from among my own people." Eliezer did as he was told. After a long journey he entered the town square. Eliezer stopped at the well.

Each evening the women would gather at the well. They would come to fill their jars full of water. "I will stay here and watch these women. Maybe God will give me a sign. Maybe one of them is the woman I am looking for," thought Eliezer.

Eliezer waited a long time. Then, a pretty, young woman came to the well. She saw Eliezer.

"You look thirsty. Would you like a drink?" she asked him.

"Yes, please," he answered.

"Are those your camels?" she asked. Eliezer nodded.

"I will give them water also," she said, as she filled her jar again.

When she had finished Eliezer called her over to him.

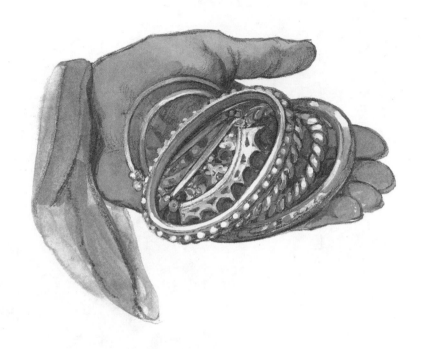

"You are a good, kind young woman. I think you are the one I am seeking." With that, Eliezer reached inside his robe and brought out a pair of earrings and four bracelets. They were made of the finest gold. He gave them to the woman. "What is your name?" he asked. "I am Rebekah," she answered.

"Please go and tell your father that I wish to speak with him," Eliezer said quietly.

That night, Eliezer met with Rebekah's father. Eliezer told him about Isaac, Abraham and the land of Canaan. He asked for Rebekah's hand in marriage to Isaac.

After much thought, Rebekah's father agreed. Eliezer's camels were loaded for the long journey back to Canaan. Rebekah kissed her father for the last time. But, she was not sad. Somehow, she knew that she would be happy with Isaac.

After many days, they arrived in Canaan. Isaac saw them coming and ran out to greet them. He loved Rebekah from the moment he saw her. She loved him too. They were married shortly after.

In due time, they had twin sons, Jacob and Esau. Jacob's children would become the founders of the twelve tribes of Israel.

All these appear in the pages of the story. Can you find them?

Rebekah and Isaac

Sarah

Abraham

Eliezer

Jacob and Esau

Now tell the story in your own words.